Kids can bake!

for kids and adults who love to bake together

Nicola Graimes

First published in 2009
Love Food ® is an imprint of Parragon Books Ltd

Parragon
Queen Street House
4 Queen Street
Bath BA1 1HE, UK

ISBN: 978-1-4075-6426-5

Printed in China

Written by Nicola Graimes
Photography by Clive Streeter
Food styling by Angela Drake
Casting by Nancy Mcdougall
Designed by Seamonster Design

With a special thank you to Benita, Adelina, Ilaria, and Gianluca Benedetto; A'liyah, Reem,
and Taybah Loghdey; Caprice and Raven Nelson; and Che and Solomon Ove-Loncraine.

Notes for the Reader
This book uses imperial, metric, and US cup measurements. Follow the same units of
measurement throughout; do not mix imperial and metric. All spoon measurements are
level: teaspoons are assumed to be 5 ml, and tablespoons are assumed to be 15 ml.
Unless otherwise stated, milk is assumed to be whole, eggs and individual vegetables are
medium, and pepper is freshly ground black pepper.

The times given are an approximate guide only. Preparation times differ according to the
techniques used by different people and the cooking times may also vary from those
given. Optional ingredients, variations, or serving suggestions have not been included in
the calculations.

Recipes using raw or very lightly cooked eggs should be avoided by infants, the elderly,
pregnant women, convalescents, and anyone with a chronic illness. Pregnant and
breastfeeding women are advised to avoid eating peanuts and peanut products. People
with nut allergies should be aware that some of the prepared ingredients used in the
recipes in this book may contain nuts. Always check the packaging before use.

Contents

Cooking together

Cooking is fun and it's even more fun if you can do it with someone else. All the recipes in this book have been created for you—the "head chef"—to cook with an adult—"kitchen assistant"—with plenty of yummy results. Cooking is about having fun, learning, and experimenting, and there are plenty of ideas here for you to try, from cookies and cakes to tarts and breads. You can make a note of your cooking successes in the Recipe Record Chart on page 10—get your family and friends to give you marks out of 10.

Before you start...

There are a few guidelines and important rules to remember when you are cooking. The following tips will make sure your recipes taste great and work every time.

1 Read the recipe before you start. Try to get all your ingredients ready and make sure you have the equipment listed at hand.

2 Wash your hands before you start cooking. Roll up your sleeves and put on an apron to protect your clothes. Tie your hair back if it is long.

3 For successful results, be careful when measuring your ingredients and always use standard kitchen measuring equipment. Measure dry ingredients with measuring cups and use a measuring pitcher or spoon for liquids.

Cooking tips

Using the recipes

The recipes in this book are graded with stars, meaning that some are more difficult than others:

★ = easy

★★ = medium

★★★ = more difficult

The recipes also have symbols to help you. Look out for:

 Makes/Serves

 Preparation time

 Cooking time

 Oven temperature

If you see the 👨‍👧 symbol, it means you need to ask an adult to help you. This could be because you need to use a hot oven or burner, or an electrical appliance, sharp knife, or scissors.

Each recipe comes with full instructions, but it is also worth remembering to:

- Turn the oven on around 15 minutes before it is needed to preheat it. It is important that the oven is at the correct temperature when baking. Use the middle shelf.

- Prepare your cake pan or baking sheet before you start. Always use the size stated in the recipe.

- Be careful when weighing and measuring your ingredients. Some food items, such as fruit and vegetables, need weighing on scales in the store. Use measuring cups for dry ingredients, and use a measuring pitcher or spoon for liquids. This is particularly important when baking.

Safe cooking!

- Always ask an adult first before starting to cook and be extra careful when handling anything hot, sharp, or electrical.

- Always wear oven mitts when handling hot baking sheets, pans, and dishes.

- When stirring food in a pan, hold the handle firmly to keep it steady.

- Turn pan handles to the side, away from the heat, so they aren't accidentally knocked off the burner.

- Wipe up any spills on the floor to prevent slipping.

- Do not walk around the kitchen with a sharp knife in your hand.

- Remember to switch off the burner or oven when you have finished cooking.

Clean and tidy

- Always wash your hands before you start to cook.

- Store raw food separately from cooked food in the refrigerator.

- Make sure that the ingredients you use have not passed their "expiration" date.

- Wipe down counters and any other work surfaces after use.

Essential equipment

1 saucepans
2 colander
3 cake pan
4 muffin pan
5 baking sheet
6 mixing bowl

7 strainer
8 measuring pitcher
9 lemon squeezer
10 rolling pin
11 oven mitts
12 wire rack

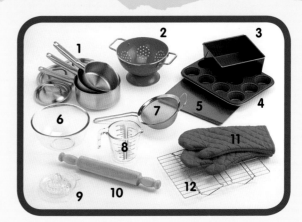

1 electric blender
2 weighing scales
3 food processor
4 grater
5 tongs
6 electric handheld mixer

7 beaters
8 storage container
9 electric handheld blender
10 balloon whisk

1 measuring cups
2 pastry brush
3 flour sifter
4 plastic spatula
5 slotted spoon
6 metal spatula
7 scissors
8 sharp knives

9 cutting board
10 garlic press
11 pastry cutter
12 vegetable peeler
13 wooden skewers
14 wooden spoon
15 wooden spatula

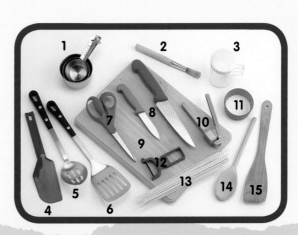

How to...

Here are some useful cookery words and tips:

Greasing a baking sheet or cake pan

To stop cookies or cakes from sticking during cooking, dip a crumpled piece of foil or parchment paper lightly into butter or oil and rub over a baking sheet or the inside of a cake pan.

Rubbing in

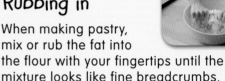

When making pastry, mix or rub the fat into the flour with your fingertips until the mixture looks like fine breadcrumbs.

Lining a cake pan or baking sheet

To stop cakes or cookies from sticking during cooking, trace around a baking sheet or pan onto parchment paper, cut just inside the line with scissors, and place on the sheet or in the pan. Remember to grease the sides of the pan, too.

Whisking

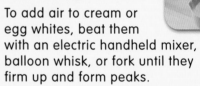

To add air to cream or egg whites, beat them with an electric handheld mixer, balloon whisk, or fork until they firm up and form peaks.

Folding in

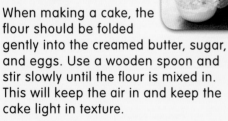

When making a cake, the flour should be folded gently into the creamed butter, sugar, and eggs. Use a wooden spoon and stir slowly until the flour is mixed in. This will keep the air in and keep the cake light in texture.

Creaming

To add air to cakes, beat the butter and sugar together with an electric handheld mixer or wooden spoon until they are light and creamy in texture.

Sifting

Put the flour (and baking powder, cocoa powder, or salt, for example) into a strainer and tap the side with the palm of your hand to help the flour pass through into a bowl below. Or use a special flour sifter. Sifting will remove any lumps and add air.

Separating eggs

Crack the egg, pull open the shell with your fingers, and let it plop into a bowl. Put an eggcup over the yolk and pour the white into another bowl.

Kneading

Put the dough on a lightly floured surface and form into a round shape. Place the heel of your hand on top of the dough and push it away from you. With your fingers fold the dough over toward you, then give it a quarter turn. Repeat for about 10 minutes, until the dough is smooth.

Rolling out pastry

Lightly flour the work surface and rolling pin, then roll out the pastry away from you in gentle movements, turning it from time to time, until it makes a thin sheet.

Juicing citrus fruit

Place the fruit on its side on a cutting board and cut in half. Place each half over the cone of a lemon squeezer, press down, and twist so that the juice goes into the base. Strain the juice through a strainer to remove the seeds.

Melting chocolate

Put the bowl of chocolate pieces over a pan of gently simmering water—but make sure the bowl does not touch the water under it—until melted.

Recipe record chart

Recipe	Date cooked	Who for?	Marks out of 10

Recipe record chart

Recipe	Date cooked	Who for?	Marks out of 10

Yummy cookies

Treat your family and friends to these scrumptious cookies. Don't forget to ask an adult to help you in the kitchen, and you will have loads of fun making the sparkly star-shape cookies, funny face lollipop cookies, and decorated gingerbread animals. Cookies make great presents, too—wrap them in clear plastic bags and tie with a colorful ribbon, or pack them into a pretty box.

makes: 10

prep: 20 minutes, plus cooling

cooking: 18 minutes

oven temp: 350°F/180°C

Fruit 'n' nut cookies

These granola-style cookies are a healthy mix of oats, dried fruit, and nuts. They are great for putting into lunch boxes or for a tasty after-school snack.

Equipment:

- scissors
- large mixing bowl
- wooden spoon
- small saucepan
- tablespoon
- 2 baking sheets, lightly greased
- wire cooling rack

What you need:

½ cup dried apricots

scant ¾ cup all-purpose flour

scant ¾ cup rolled oats

½ cup chopped hazelnuts

9 tbsp unsalted butter, cut into small pieces

generous ⅓ cup light brown sugar

2 tbsp dark corn syrup

1 Preheat the oven. Cut the apricots into small pieces using scissors.

2 Put the apricots in a large bowl with the flour, oats, and hazelnuts. Using a wooden spoon, stir until mixed together.

3 Put the butter, brown sugar, and corn syrup in a saucepan and heat gently, stirring from time to time, until melted.

4 Pour the butter mixture into the bowl and stir to make a soft, chunky dough.

5 Place heaping spoonfuls of the dough onto the baking sheets and flatten the tops, until about 2 inches/5 cm wide and ½ inch/1 cm thick. Leave space between the cookies so they can spread.

6 Bake for 15 minutes, until light golden. Remove from the oven and let the cookies cool a little, then move them to a wire rack to cool and become crispy.

makes: about 20

 prep: 15 minutes, plus cooling

 cooking: 15–20 minutes

oven temp: 350°F/180°C

Sparkly stars

These cinnamon-spiced cookies look fantastic decorated with icing and sparkly silver balls. Let the icing thicken slightly before spreading it over the stars.

Equipment:

- strainer or flour sifter
- large mixing bowl
- wooden spoon
- rolling pin
- star-shape cutter
- 2 large baking sheets, lined with parchment paper
- wire cooling rack
- small mixing bowl
- teaspoon

What you need:

1½ cups all-purpose flour
1 tsp baking powder
pinch of salt
⅔ cup unsalted butter, cut into small pieces
generous ½ cup light brown sugar
1 tsp ground cinnamon
1 egg yolk
1¾ cups confectioners' sugar

1 tbsp lemon juice
½–1 tbsp water
edible silver balls

1 Preheat the oven. Sift the flour, baking powder, and salt into a large bowl and stir with a wooden spoon until combined. Add the butter.

2 Rub in the butter using your fingertips until the mixture looks like fine breadcrumbs. Stir in the brown sugar, cinnamon, and egg yolk.

3 Use your hands to make a soft dough. Lightly flour the work surface and rolling pin, then roll out the dough until it is about ¼ inch/5 mm thick.

4 Use a star-shape cutter to stamp out 20 cookies, then carefully place 10 cookies on each baking sheet.

5 Bake in the oven for 15–20 minutes. Remove from the oven and let the cookies cool a little on the sheets, then move to a wire rack.

6 Put the confectioners' sugar in a small bowl and add the lemon juice. Stir in the water a little at a time to make a smooth icing. Spread over each cookie with the back of a teaspoon, then decorate with silver balls.

Gingerbread animals

There are many different animal cutters to choose from—everything from snails to lions. Pick your favorite, or perhaps choose a theme, such as "pets" or "zoo animals."

makes: about 10 (depending on the size of the cutter)

prep: 15 minutes, plus cooling/chilling

cooking: 12–15 minutes

oven temp: 375°F/190°C

What you need:

1¼ cups all-purpose flour, plus extra if needed

2 tsp ground ginger

½ tsp baking soda

4 tbsp unsalted butter, cut into small pieces

scant ½ cup light brown sugar

2 tbsp dark corn syrup

1 egg, lightly beaten

tubes of decorating icing in different colors, to decorate

Equipment:

- strainer or flour sifter
- large mixing bowl
- small saucepan
- wooden spoon
- plastic wrap
- rolling pin
- animal-shape cutters
- large baking sheet, lined with parchment paper
- wire cooling rack

1 Sift the flour, ginger, and baking soda into a large bowl. Rub in the butter using your fingertips until the mixture looks like fine breadcrumbs.

2 Gently heat the brown sugar and corn syrup in a saucepan until melted. Pour into the bowl, then add the egg.

3 Mix with a wooden spoon to make a soft dough. If it is too sticky, add a little more flour and mix again. Wrap in plastic wrap and chill for 30 minutes. Preheat the oven.

4 Lightly flour the work surface and rolling pin, then unwrap the dough and roll out until it is about ¼ inch/5 mm thick. Use cutters to stamp out about 10 animal shapes, rerolling the dough as necessary.

5 Carefully place the cookies on the baking sheet and bake for 12–15 minutes, until just crispy. Remove from the oven and let cool a little on the sheet.

6 Move the cookies to a wire rack. When cool, decorate with the tubes of icing.

makes: 19

prep: 15 minutes, plus cooling

cooking: 10–12 minutes

oven temp: 350°F/180°C

Button cookies

These button-shape cookies can be threaded onto colored ribbons to make pretty party decorations.

Equipment:

- strainer or flour sifter
- large mixing bowl
- wooden spoon
- rolling pin
- 2½-inch/6-cm round cutter
- 2 large baking sheets, greased
- palette knife
- skewer
- wire cooling rack

What you need:

1¾ cups all-purpose flour

3 tbsp cornstarch

generous ⅓ cup superfine sugar

¾ cup unsalted butter, cut into small pieces

1–2 tsp milk

thin ribbons, to decorate

1 Preheat the oven. Sift the flour, cornstarch, and superfine sugar into a large bowl. Rub in the butter, using your fingertips, to make a soft, buttery mixture.

2 Stir in the milk using a wooden spoon, then bring the mixture together with your hands to make a dough.

3 Lightly flour the work surface and rolling pin. Knead the dough gently until smooth, then roll out until it is about ¼ inch/5 mm thick.

4 Use a round cutter to stamp out 19 circles, rerolling the dough as necessary. Carefully lift onto the baking sheets using a palette knife.

5 Use a skewer to make 4 holes in each cookie, so it looks like a button, turning the skewer to make the holes big enough to thread the ribbon through.

6 Bake in the oven for 10–12 minutes, until pale golden. Remove from the oven and let the cookies cool a little, then move to a wire rack. When cool, thread the ribbons through the holes and tie the ends into a bow.

21

★★★

Funny face lollipops

Have fun making these cookies—try different faces and expressions using tubes of decorating icing. The sticks can be found in special kitchen shops.

WARNING Ice-cream sticks can be dangerous and children should be encouraged not to run around while eating their lollipop cookies.

makes: 8

 prep: 15 minutes, plus cooling/chilling

 cooking: 20–25 minutes

 oven temp: 350°F/180°C

What you need:

½ cup unsalted butter, cut into small pieces, softened
generous ⅓ cup superfine sugar
1 tsp vanilla extract
1 egg yolk
scant 1½ cups all-purpose flour
tubes of decorating icing in different colors, to decorate

Equipment:

- large mixing bowl
- electric handheld mixer
- strainer or flour sifter
- wooden spoon
- plastic wrap
- 8 wooden ice-cream sticks
- rolling pin
- 3¼-inch/8-cm round cutter
- 2 large baking sheets, lined with parchment paper
- wire cooling rack

1 Put the butter and superfine sugar in a large bowl and beat with an electric mixer until pale and fluffy—this will take about 5 minutes.

2 Add the vanilla extract and egg yolk and beat again on a low speed. Sift in the flour and fold in with a wooden spoon.

3 Mix well, but gently, to make a smooth, creamy dough. Wrap the dough in plastic wrap and chill for 30 minutes.

4 Meanwhile, soak the ice-cream sticks in water for 30 minutes. This stops them from burning when they are baked. Preheat the oven.

5 Lightly flour the work surface and rolling pin. Unwrap the dough and roll out until about ⅓ inch/7 mm thick. Use a round cutter to stamp out 8 cookies, rerolling the dough as necessary. Carefully insert a stick into each cookie.

6 Place 4 cookies on each baking sheet and bake for 20–25 minutes, until light golden. Remove from the oven and let the cookies cool a little, then move to a wire rack. When cool, pipe faces on the cookies using tubes of decorating icing.

23

24

Cakes galore

There's something here for everyone and every occasion, from dainty little butterfly cakes to a big chocolate birthday cake. Have fun decorating the birthday cake with your cooking assistant—and don't forget the candles! There are also recipes for a creamy frosting-topped carrot cake (no one will guess it has carrots in it!) and a deliciously fruity tropical banana bread.

makes: 12

 prep: 15 minutes, plus cooling

 cooking: 20–25 minutes

 oven temp: 400°F/200°C

Strawberry explosion muffins

It's not until you bite into these delicious muffins that you discover the secret strawberry jelly filling inside.

Equipment:

- strainer or flour sifter
- large mixing bowl
- wooden spoon
- measuring pitcher
- balloon whisk or fork
- tablespoon
- deep muffin pan, lined with 12 paper liners
- teaspoon
- wire cooling rack
- small mixing bowl

What you need:

1²/₃ cups all-purpose flour
1 tsp baking powder
¾ cup superfine sugar
generous ⅓ cup milk
2 large eggs
⅔ cup unsalted butter, melted
12 tsp strawberry jelly

Buttercream:
3 tbsp unsalted butter, softened
scant ½ cup confectioners' sugar
½ tsp vanilla extract
1–2 tsp milk

6 strawberries, halved, to decorate

1 Preheat the oven. Sift the flour and baking powder into a large bowl. Stir in the superfine sugar using a wooden spoon.

2 Put the milk, eggs, and butter in a pitcher and whisk together with a balloon whisk or fork. Pour a little at a time into the bowl, stirring gently until combined.

3 Spoon a heaping tablespoon of the muffin mixture into each paper liner, then add a teaspoonful of jelly. Top with the rest of the muffin mixture.

4 Bake in the oven for 20–25 minutes, until risen. Remove from the oven and let the muffins cool a little, then move to a wire rack.

5 To make the buttercream, put the butter, confectioners' sugar, vanilla extract, and milk in a small bowl and beat together until smooth and creamy.

6 Place a spoonful of the buttercream on top of each muffin, then decorate with a strawberry half.

Butterfly cakes

What would a party be without cakes? You will love decorating these little cupcakes, and your friends will love eating them!

makes: 12

 prep: 10 minutes, plus cooling

 cooking: 12–15 minutes

 oven temp: 350°F/180°C

What you need:

⅔ cup unsalted butter, cut into small pieces, softened
¾ cup superfine sugar
½ tsp vanilla extract
2 large eggs, lightly beaten
1 cup self-rising flour, sifted
1–2 tbsp milk

Buttercream:

6 tbsp unsalted butter, softened
1½ cups confectioners' sugar
1 tbsp orange juice

colored sprinkles, to decorate

Equipment:

- large mixing bowl
- electric handheld mixer
- wooden spoon
- tablespoon
- muffin pan, lined with 12 paper liners
- wire cooling rack
- small serrated knife
- medium mixing bowl

1 Preheat the oven. In a large bowl, beat the butter and superfine sugar, using an electric mixer, until the mixture is pale and fluffy—this takes about 5 minutes.

2 Add the vanilla extract and 1 of the eggs and beat on a low speed. Beat in a spoonful of flour, then the second egg and the milk.

3 Fold in the rest of the flour using a wooden spoon to make a smooth mixture.

4 Using a tablespoon, spoon the mixture into the paper liners. Bake in the oven for 12–15 minutes, until risen and golden. Remove from the oven, let cool a little, then move to a wire rack.

5 When cool, slice off the top of each cake and cut in half to make butterfly wings. For the buttercream, beat together the butter, confectioners' sugar, and orange juice.

6 Place a spoonful of buttercream on top of each cupcake, scatter over the sprinkles. Place the wings on top.

★★

makes: 12 slices

prep: 25 minutes, plus cooling

cooking: 50–60 minutes

oven temp: 350°F/180°C

Tropical banana bread

This rich, moist cake is full of fruit and is great cut into slices and packed into a lunch box. Very ripe bananas will give the best flavor.

Equipment:

- medium mixing bowl
- fork
- strainer or flour sifter
- large mixing bowl
- wooden spoon
- 9 x 5 x 3-inch/23 x 13 x 8-cm loaf pan, greased and lined
- wire cooling rack

What you need:

5 ripe bananas (2¼ cups when mashed—see step 1 below)
scant 1½ cups white self-rising flour
⅓ cup whole wheat self-rising flour
1 tsp baking powder
9 tbsp unsalted butter, cut into small pieces, chilled

3 large eggs, lightly beaten
½ cup superfine sugar
½ cup chopped, plumped dried tropical fruit mix
confectioners' sugar, for dusting

1 Preheat the oven. Break the bananas up into a medium bowl, then mash them with a fork until almost smooth.

2 Sift both types of flour and the baking powder into a large bowl, tipping in any bran left in the strainer or sifter, then add the butter.

3 Using your fingertips, rub the butter into the flour mixture until it looks like fine breadcrumbs.

4 Stir in the eggs, superfine sugar, bananas, and dried fruit, using a wooden spoon, then pour into the loaf pan.

5 Level the top using the back of the spoon, then bake for about 50–60 minutes, until risen and golden.

6 Remove from the oven and let the cake cool in the pan for 10 minutes, then turn out onto a wire rack. Dust with confectioners' sugar before slicing.

Carrot cake squares

makes: 16 squares

prep: 15 minutes, plus cooling/chilling

cooking: 50 minutes

oven temp: 350°F/180°C

No one will ever guess that this delicious cake is made from carrots! It is one of the easiest cakes to make—no creaming or beating—but it is still light and moist with a yummy creamy topping.

Equipment:

- strainer or flour sifter
- large mixing bowl
- wooden spoon
- 8-inch/20-cm square cake pan, greased and lined with parchment paper
- wire cooling rack
- medium mixing bowl
- palette knife
- large knife

What you need:

¾ cup whole wheat self-rising flour
1 cup white self-rising flour
1 tsp baking powder
2 tsp ground allspice
1¼ cups dark brown sugar
4 medium carrots (about 9 oz/250 g), peeled and grated
3 large eggs, lightly beaten
scant 1 cup sunflower oil

Frosting:

⅔ cup low-fat cream cheese
4 tbsp unsalted butter, softened
1 tsp vanilla extract
1½ cups confectioners' sugar

yellow, red, and green rolled fondant, to decorate

1 Preheat the oven. Sift both types of flour into a large bowl, tipping in any bran left in the strainer. Using a wooden spoon, stir in the baking powder, allspice, brown sugar, and carrots.

2 Add the eggs and oil, then stir until mixed together. Pour the mixture into the pan and smooth the top with the back of the spoon.

3 Bake for 50 minutes, until golden. Remove from the oven and let cool for 10 minutes, then place a wire rack on top and carefully turn out the cake.

4 When the cake is cool, beat the cream cheese, butter, vanilla extract, and confectioners' sugar in a medium bowl until smooth and creamy. Chill in the refrigerator for 10 minutes.

5 Spread the frosting over the cake and smooth using a palette knife, then cut into 16 squares.

6 Mix together the yellow and red fondant to make orange. Roll into 16 carrot shapes. Top each "carrot" with a small piece of green fondant, then place 1 on top of each square.

★ ★ ★

Big chocolate birthday cake

Your friends will love this delicious chocolate cake and it's also really fun to make. Try using different cake decorations to create your own special version.

makes: 15 slices

 prep: 20 minutes, plus cooling

 cooking: 25 minutes

 oven temp: 350°F/180°C

What you need:

1⅓ cups self-rising flour, sifted
½ cup unsweetened cocoa, sifted
1 cup superfine sugar
1 cup unsalted butter,
   cut into small pieces, softened
4 large eggs, lightly beaten

Frosting:
7 oz/200 g milk chocolate,
   broken into squares
1¾ oz/50 g semisweet chocolate,
   broken into squares
1 cup heavy cream

sugar-coated chocolate candies,
   to decorate

Equipment:

- large mixing bowl
- electric handheld mixer
- two 8-inch/20-cm round
  cake pans, greased and lined
- wooden spoon
- wire cooling rack
- medium heatproof bowl
- medium saucepan
- palette knife

1 Preheat the oven. Put the flour, cocoa, superfine sugar, butter, and eggs into a large bowl. Using an electric mixer, beat for 2 minutes, until smooth and creamy.

2 Divide the mixture evenly between the 2 cake pans and smooth the tops with the back of a wooden spoon.

3 Bake for 25 minutes, until risen. Remove from the oven and let cool in the pans for 10 minutes, then turn out onto a wire rack.

4 For the frosting, put both chocolates in a heatproof bowl placed over a saucepan holding 1 inch/2.5 cm of water—make sure the bowl does not touch the water.

5 Bring the water to a simmer. Melt the chocolate, stirring once or twice. Carefully remove the bowl from the pan. Stir the cream into the melted chocolate and let cool and thicken.

6 Sandwich the two cakes together with some of the chocolate frosting, then spread the rest over the top and sides of the cake with a palette knife. Decorate with chocolate candies.

35

Afternoon treats

Your cooking assistant won't need much persuading to join you in making these scrummy afternoon treats! You'll both have loads of fun preparing jelly-filled tarts, meringue clouds, chocolate honeycomb brownies, and the rock 'n' roll cakes with chunks of chocolate and gooey marshmallow. Of course, you don't have to save them just for an afternoon snack.

makes: 12

prep: 10 minutes,
plus cooling

cooking:
15–18 minutes

oven temp:
350°F/180°C

Rock 'n' roll cakes

These are rock cakes with a difference as they contain chunks of chocolate and gooey marshmallows. Simple to make, they take just minutes to put together.

Equipment:

- large mixing bowl
- wooden spoon
- measuring pitcher
- balloon whisk or fork
- tablespoon
- 2 baking sheets, lined with parchment paper
- wire cooling rack

What you need:

6 tbsp unsalted butter, cut into small pieces
scant 2¼ cups self-rising flour
generous ⅓ cup superfine sugar
1¼ cups mini white marshmallows
2¾ oz/75 g milk chocolate chunks

⅔ cup milk
1 large egg
1 tsp vanilla extract

1 Preheat the oven. In a large bowl, rub the butter into the flour with your fingertips until the mixture looks like fine breadcrumbs.

2 Stir in the superfine sugar, mini marshmallows, and chocolate chunks with a wooden spoon until evenly mixed together.

3 Put the milk, egg, and vanilla extract in a pitcher and whisk together with a balloon whisk or fork.

4 Pour the mixture into the bowl and stir to make a chunky cake mixture.

5 For each rock cake, place 2 heaped tablespoons of the mixture on a baking sheet. Repeat to make 12 rock cakes in total.

6 Bake in the oven for 15–18 minutes, until pale golden. Remove from the oven and let the rock cakes cool a little, then move to a wire rack.

Cherry biscuits

Delicious topped with butter and jelly, there's nothing nicer than warm homemade biscuits. If you can't find buttermilk, replace it with the same amount of plain yogurt mixed with 1 tablespoon of lemon juice.

makes: 8

 prep: 10 minutes, plus cooling

 cooking: 12–15 minutes, plus cooling

oven temp: 400°F/200°C

What you need:

2 cups self-rising flour

pinch of salt

4 tbsp unsalted butter, cut into small pieces

1½ tbsp superfine sugar

2 eggs, lightly beaten

2/3 cup buttermilk

scant ½ cup plumped dried cherries

Equipment:

- strainer or flour sifter
- large mixing bowl
- wooden spoon
- 2½-inch/6-cm round cutter
- large baking sheet, dusted with flour
- wire cooling rack

1 Preheat the oven. Sift the flour and salt into a large bowl. Rub in the butter with your fingertips until the mixture looks like fine breadcrumbs.

2 Gently stir in the superfine sugar, eggs, buttermilk, and cherries with a wooden spoon, then press the mixture together to make a soft dough.

3 Lightly flour a work surface, tip the dough out of the bowl, and knead gently to make a smooth ball.

4 Press the top of the dough down with the palm of your hand until it makes a 1-inch/ 2.5-cm thick round shape. Be gentle with the dough or the biscuits will be heavy.

5 Use a round cutter to stamp out 8 circles, then place them on the baking sheet.

6 Bake the biscuits for 12–15 minutes, until light golden and risen. Remove from the oven and let the biscuits cool a little, then move to a wire rack.

Queen of tarts

Everyone loves tarts! You can fill them with your favorite jelly or jam, or maybe try using several different jellies to create a colorful mixture.

makes: 12

 prep: 15 minutes, plus cooling/ chilling

 cooking: 20 minutes

 oven temp: 375°F/190°C

What you need:

7 tbsp unsalted butter, cut into small pieces, chilled
scant 1½ cups all-purpose flour
2 tbsp superfine sugar
1 egg yolk, lightly beaten
12 tbsp jelly of your choice

Equipment:

• large mixing bowl
• wooden spoon
• plastic wrap
• rolling pin
• round cutter
• muffin pan, 12 holes greased
• tablespoon
• wire cooling rack

1 In a large bowl, rub the butter into the flour with your fingertips until the mixture looks like fine breadcrumbs.

2 Stir in the superfine sugar and then the egg yolk with a wooden spoon until the mixture comes together— you might need to add a little cold water.

3 Wrap the pastry in plastic wrap and chill for 30 minutes. Preheat the oven. Lightly flour the work surface, then unwrap the pastry and roll out until it is about ¼ inch/5 mm thick.

4 Stamp out circles of pastry large enough to fit into the holes of the muffin pan. Press a circle of pastry into each hole.

5 Bake the pastry shells for 15 minutes, then carefully remove from the oven. Add a tablespoonful of jelly to each shell.

6 Bake for another 5 minutes. Remove from the oven and let the tarts cool a little, then move to a wire rack.

★ ★ ★

Chocolate honeycomb brownies

Your family and friends will love these yummy chocolate brownies with chunks of honeycomb. Cut into small squares and eat warm either on their own or with vanilla ice cream.

makes: 16

 prep: 20 minutes, plus cooling

 cooking: 35–40 minutes

 oven temp: 350°F/180°C

What you need:

9 tbsp unsalted butter, cut into small pieces

3½ oz/100 g semisweet chocolate, broken into squares

2 large eggs

generous 1⅓ cups superfine sugar

⅔ cup all-purpose flour

1 tsp baking powder

2 tbsp unsweetened cocoa

2¾ oz/80 g honeycomb or chocolate-coated honeycomb, broken into large chunks

Equipment:

- medium heatproof bowl
- medium saucepan
- wooden spoon
- large mixing bowl
- electric handheld mixer
- strainer or flour sifter
- 8-inch/20-cm square cake pan, greased and lined
- knife

1 Preheat the oven. Put the butter and chocolate in a heatproof bowl placed over a pan holding 1 inch/2.5 cm of water—make sure the bowl does not touch the water.

2 Bring the water to a simmer and melt the butter and chocolate, stirring once or twice. Carefully remove from the heat and let cool a little.

3 In a large mixing bowl, beat the eggs and superfine sugar using an electric handheld mixer for 5 minutes, until pale and fluffy. Stir in the melted chocolate mixture.

4 Sift the flour, baking powder, and cocoa into the bowl, and fold in until mixed together.

5 Fold the honeycomb into the chocolate mixture, then pour into the cake pan and level the top using the back of the spoon.

6 Bake in the oven for 35–40 minutes, until risen but a bit soft in the center. Remove from the oven. Let cool in the pan a little. Turn out and cut into 16 squares.

★★★

 makes: 10

 prep: 15 minutes,
plus cooling

 cooking:
1 hour 10 minutes

oven temp:
350°F/180°C

Meringue clouds

Light and fluffy like clouds, these meringues are topped with a sweet, creamy topping and fresh strawberries but they are just as good served plain.

Equipment:

- 3¼-inch/8-cm round cutter
- 2 sheets of parchment paper (to fit the baking sheets)
- pencil
- 2 baking sheets
- 2 large mixing bowls
- electric handheld mixer
- tablespoon
- wire cooling rack

What you need:

4 egg whites
1½ cups superfine sugar
2 tsp white wine vinegar
2 tsp cornstarch
1¼ cups heavy cream
4 tbsp confectioners' sugar
1 tsp vanilla extract
1 lb 2 oz/500 g strawberries, hulled and halved if large

1 Preheat the oven. Place a round cutter on top of a sheet of parchment paper and carefully trace around it with a pencil. Repeat until you have 5 circles on each sheet and put, drawn-side down, on the baking sheets.

2 Put the egg whites in a large bowl, then beat using an electric handheld mixer until the egg whites stand in firm, stiff peaks.

3 Whisk in the superfine sugar a tablespoonful at a time until the mixture is shiny and stiff, then whisk in the vinegar and cornstarch.

46

4 Spoon the mixture onto the circles on the parchment paper and make dips in the center of each with the back of the spoon.

5 Bake for 10 minutes, then turn the oven down to 250°F/120°C and cook for 1 hour. Remove from the oven and let the meringues cool a little, then move to a wire rack.

6 Whisk together the cream, confectioners' sugar, and vanilla extract in another large bowl until the mixture stands in soft peaks. Spoon the cream into the dips in the meringues and top with strawberries.

Savory selection

Feeling peckish? Ask your cooking partner to help you to make these tasty tummy fillers. There are ideas for all kinds of occasion, from tasty snacks to party treats and lunch-box fillers. If you haven't made bread before, try our simple recipe and fill your home with the delicious smell of a freshly baked loaf.

makes: 1 loaf

 prep: 15 minutes, plus cooling

 cooking: 35–40 minutes

 oven temp: 400°F/200°C

My first bread

If you haven't made bread before, soda bread is the perfect place to start. It's quick to make because it doesn't need time for rising, but it is still delicious, especially eaten warm!

Equipment:

- strainer or flour sifter
- large mixing bowl
- knife
- fork
- baking sheet, dusted with flour
- wire cooling rack

What you need:

3¼ cups all-purpose flour
  (white or whole wheat)
1 tsp salt
1 tsp baking soda
generous 1 cup buttermilk
  (or 1 cup plain yogurt
  mixed with 1 tablespoon
  lemon juice)
2 tbsp plain yogurt

1 Preheat the oven. Sift the flour, salt, and baking soda into a large bowl. Make a well in the center of the flour mixture.

2 Pour the buttermilk into the well, then gently mix with your fingers to make a soft, slightly sticky dough. If the dough is too dry, add the yogurt.

3 Lightly flour the work surface, then gently knead the dough into a smooth ball—don't knead too much, or the dough will become tough.

50

4 Press the top of the dough down with the palm of your hand to make a round loaf about 2 inches/5 cm thick.

5 Use a knife to cut a deep cross into the top of the dough—and prick each quarter so the "fairies can get out." Put the loaf on the baking sheet.

6 Sift a little flour over the top and bake in the oven for 35–40 minutes, until risen and golden. Remove from the oven and move to a wire rack to cool.

makes: 18

prep: 20 minutes,
plus cooling

cooking:
25–30 minutes

oven temp:
350°F/180°C

Cockadoodle rolls

These homemade chicken rolls make a change from hot dogs and hamburgers and can be eaten warm or cold.

Equipment:

- large mixing bowl
- tablespoon
- sharp knife
- pastry brush
- 2 large baking sheets, greased
- fork
- wire cooling rack

What you need:

9 oz/250 g ground chicken or turkey
1 small onion, grated
1 small carrot, peeled and grated
½ cup fresh breadcrumbs
1 tsp dried mixed herbs
1 tsp Dijon mustard
1 egg, lightly beaten

7½ oz/215 g store-bought puff pastry sheet, defrosted if frozen
milk, for brushing
salt and pepper

1 Preheat the oven. Put the ground meat, onion, carrot, breadcrumbs, herbs, mustard, and egg into a large bowl. Season with salt and pepper. Mix together with a tablespoon.

2 Lightly flour the work surface, then place the pastry sheet on it. Cut crosswise into 3 rectangles.

3 Spoon a sausage shape of the meat mixture along the long side of 1 of the pastry rectangles, about 1 inch/ 2.5 cm in from the edge.

4 Brush the edge of the pastry with milk and roll it tightly over the meat mixture. Press the edges together to make a long sausage roll shape.

5 Cut the roll into 6. Repeat the steps with the other 2 pastry rectangles and the rest of the meat mixture. Place on the baking sheets.

6 Brush each roll with milk and prick with a fork. Bake for 25–30 minutes, until golden. Remove from the oven and move to a wire rack to cool.

Mini bacon and cheese tarts

Amaze your family with these mini quiches, which look fantastic when they come out of the oven all risen and golden!

makes: 6

 prep: 20 minutes, plus cooling/chilling

 cooking: 28–33 minutes

 oven temp: 400°F/200°C

What you need:

3 slices lean smoked bacon

7 oz/200 g store-bought puff pastry sheet, defrosted if frozen

2 eggs, beaten

generous ¼ cup milk

½ cup grated sharp cheddar cheese

1 tomato, sliced into circles

salt and pepper

Equipment:

- scissors
- round cutter
- deep muffin pan, 6 holes greased
- small mixing bowl
- fork
- wire cooling rack

1 Heat the broiler to high, then broil the bacon for 8 minutes, turning halfway through cooking. Let cool, then remove the rind and snip the bacon into small pieces using scissors.

2 Lightly flour the work surface, then place the pastry sheet on it. Use a round cutter to stamp out 6 circles large enough to fit into the holes of the muffin pan. Press each pastry circle into the muffin pan. Chill for 30 minutes. Preheat the oven.

3 Put the eggs and milk in a small bowl, mix together with a fork, and season with salt and pepper.

4 Sprinkle a little of the cheese and bacon into each pastry shell.

5 Pour the egg mixture into the pastry shells, filling almost to the top, then place a tomato slice on top.

6 Bake in the oven for 20–25 minutes, until risen and golden. Remove from the oven, let the tarts cool a little, then move to a wire rack.

55

Cheese moons

These cheesy cookies make great moon shapes—use a round cutter to make half moons, three-quarter moons, and full moons.

makes: 12–18

 prep: 10 minutes, plus cooling

 cooking: 10 minutes

oven temp: 400°F/200°C

What you need:

¾ cup all-purpose flour

large pinch of English mustard powder

6 tbsp unsalted butter, cut into small pieces

½ cup finely grated Parmesan cheese

1 large egg yolk

Equipment:

• strainer or flour sifter
• large mixing bowl
• fork
• rolling pin
• 2-inch/5-cm round cutter
• large baking sheet, lightly greased
• palette knife

1 Preheat the oven. Sift the flour and mustard powder into a large bowl.

2 Rub in the butter using your fingertips to make rough breadcrumbs, then stir in the Parmesan cheese with a fork.

3 Mix in the egg yolk and bring the mixture together with your hands to make a dough.

4 Lightly flour the work surface and rolling pin, then roll out the dough until it is just $1/8$ inch/3 mm thick. Use a round cutter to stamp out circles (or full moons), rerolling the dough as necessary.

5 You can make half moons and three-quarter moons by cutting away half or a quarter of each circle. Lift onto the baking sheet with a palette knife.

6 Bake for 10 minutes, until pale golden and beginning to become crispy. Remove from the oven and let cool on the baking sheet.

★ ★ ★

Caterpillar rolls

These mini bread rolls are stuck together to make a caterpillar shape. Stick on olives to make the eyes and sprinkle each roll with either sunflower or poppy seeds.

makes: 10

 prep:
10–15 minutes,
plus rising/cooling

 cooking:
20 minutes

 oven temp:
400°F/200°C

What you need:

1¾ cups white bread flour,
 plus extra if needed
1 tsp salt
1 tsp active dry yeast
¾ cup lukewarm water
1 egg yolk, beaten
1 pitted black olive, halved
sunflower seeds and poppy
 seeds, to decorate

Equipment:

- strainer or flour sifter
- large mixing bowl
- wooden spoon
- pastry brush
- large baking sheet, dusted
 with flour
- clean dish towel
- wire cooling rack

1 Sift the flour and salt into a large bowl and stir in the yeast. Make a well in the center and pour in the water. Mix to a soft dough.

2 Lightly flour the work surface, then knead the dough for 5–10 minutes, until smooth. Add a little more flour if the dough becomes sticky.

3 Divide the dough into 10 equal-size pieces and shape each piece into a ball.

4 Brush the sides of each roll with a little egg yolk and stick together on the baking sheet in the shape of a caterpillar.

5 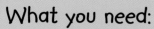 Cover with a dish towel and let stand in a warm place for 45 minutes, until the dough balls have almost doubled in size. Preheat the oven.

6 Remove the dish towel and brush the rolls with the rest of the egg yolk, then decorate with the olive and seeds. Bake for 20 minutes, then remove from the oven and move to a wire rack to cool.

★ ★ ★

makes: 2 pizzas
(serves 4–8)

prep: 20 minutes,
plus rising

cooking:
10–15 minutes

oven temp:
450°F/230°C

Pizza party

This makes 2 pizzas—perfect for a party! Each quarter of the pizza has a different topping, which means that there is something for everyone.

Equipment:

- large mixing bowl
- wooden spoon
- rolling pin
- 2 large baking sheets, dusted with flour
- small mixing bowl
- tablespoon
- pastry brush
- knife or pizza wheel

What you need:

generous 2¾ cups white bread flour
1 tsp salt
1 envelope active dry yeast
1 tbsp olive oil, plus extra for brushing
generous 1 cup lukewarm water

Tomato sauce:
1 tbsp olive oil
generous ¾ cup tomato sauce
2 tsp tomato paste
1 tsp dried oregano

Topping:
10½ oz/300 g mozzarella, torn into pieces

Plus a selection of the following:
pepperoni slices
sliced, pitted olives
ham slices
pineapple chunks
sliced vegetables, such as onions, mushrooms, or bell peppers

1 Mix together the flour, salt, and yeast in a large bowl. Make a well in the center and pour in the oil and water, then mix to make a soft dough.

2 Lightly flour the work surface and rolling pin, then knead the dough for 10 minutes, until smooth.

3 Divide the dough into 2 pieces and roll out to make 2 thin pizza bases. Put the pizza bases on the baking sheets and let stand in a warm place for 20 minutes. Preheat the oven.

4 Mix together the oil, tomato sauce, tomato paste, and oregano in a small bowl and spread thinly over the pizza bases with the back of a tablespoon.

5 Sprinkle the pizzas with the mozzarella and top each quarter with a different topping of your choice.

6 Brush the topping with oil and bake the pizzas for 10–15 minutes. Remove from the oven, then cut each pizza into 8 slices with a knife or pizza wheel.

Cooking words

Here are some cooking words that you will find in this book with simple explanations:

Bake: To cook a food/dish in the oven.

Beat: To stir or mix an ingredient energetically in order to add air.

Blend: To mix ingredients together in a food processor or blender to make a smooth mixture or liquid.

Boil: To heat a liquid, such as water, over a high heat until it bubbles.

Broil: To cook or brown food under a high heat.

Chill: To cool an ingredient or food in the refrigerator.

Chop: To cut an ingredient into smaller pieces.

Cream: To beat butter and sugar together using a wooden spoon or electric handheld mixer to add air until it is light and fluffy.

Dough: A mixture of flour, liquid, and usually other ingredients that are combined together and shaped to make cookies, bread, or pastry.

Drain: To pour off unwanted liquid, sometimes through a colander or strainer, as well as to remove excess oil after frying by placing the food on paper towels.

Drizzle: To slowly pour a trickle of liquid or sauce over a food.

Egg wash: Beaten egg used to add a shiny surface to pastry or bread after baking.

Flour: To sprinkle an ingredient, utensil, or a work surface, such as a counter, with flour.

Fold in: To mix a whisked or beaten mixture gently into another, sometimes a little at a time, to keep as much air as possible.

Fry: To cook food in oil in a skillet or saucepan over a direct heat.

Grate: To rub food, such as cheese, vegetables, or chocolate, up and down a grater over holes of different sizes to make thin or thick shreds.

Grease: To coat a baking sheet or cake pan lightly with oil or butter to stop food sticking.

Knead: To fold and press bread dough with the heel of your hand to make it smooth and stretchy.

Mash: To crush food, such as bananas or cooked potatoes, to make it smooth.

Melt: To turn a solid, such as chocolate or butter, into a liquid using heat.

Pastry: A mixture of fat, flour, and liquid and/or egg yolk to make a dough that is shaped and baked.

Peel: To remove the skin from food, such as fruit and vegetables, using a vegetable peeler or small knife.

Puree: To blend or liquidize (usually with a little water) a food, such as fruit or vegetables, until very smooth.

Rinse: To place a food under cold running water.

Rise: This is what happens when you let bread dough stand in a warm place—the dough will double in size.

Roll out: To flatten a food, such as pastry, into a smooth, even layer using a rolling pin.

Roughly chop: To cut an ingredient into pieces of different sizes.

Rub in: To mix fat, such as butter, into flour with your fingertips until the mixture looks like fine breadcrumbs.

Season: To add flavor to food using salt and pepper.

Separate eggs: To separate the yolk from the white.

Sift: To put an ingredient, such as flour, through a mesh utensil called a strainer to remove lumps and add air. Or to use a flour sifter, which has a squeezable handle.

Simmer: To cook food gently in a pan over a low direct heat, making sure it does not boil.

Slice: To cut a food into thick or thin strips or pieces.

Stir: To mix ingredients together to combine them or to prevent sticking if being cooked.

Whisk: To mix or beat ingredients quickly using an electric handheld mixer, balloon whisk, or fork in order to add air.

Index